COFFEE MORNING RECIPES

Sian Llewellyn

DOMINO

DOMINO BOOKS LTD

METRIC/IMPERIAL/AMERICAN UNITS

We are all used to doubling or halving a recipe. Thus, a Victoria sandwich may be made using 4 oz each of flour, sugar and butter with 2 eggs or 6 oz each of flour, sugar and butter with 3 eggs. The proportions of the ingredients are unchanged. This must be so for all units. Use either the metric units or the imperial units given in the recipes, do not mix the two.

It is not practical to give the exact equivalents of metric and imperial units because 1 oz equals 28.35 gm and 1 pint equals 568 ml. The tables on page 47 indicate suitable quantities but liquids should be carefully added to obtain the correct consistency. See also the charts on page iv.

PINT TO MILLILITRES AND LITRES
The following are approximations only

¼ pint = 150 ml
½ pint = 275 ml
¾ pint = 425 ml

1 pint = 568 ml (600 ml approx.)
1¾ pints = 1000 ml (1 litre)
3 pints = 1½ litres

CONTENTS

© D C P and E J P, 1990
Cover photograph by Angelo Conti
Drawings by Allison Frewtrell

ISBN 1 85122 083 6

The following charts give the approximate equivalents for metric and imperial weights, and oven temperatures.

Ounces	Approx gm to nearest whole number	Approx gm to nearest whole 25 gm
1	28	25
2	57	50
3	85	75
4	113	125
5	142	150
6	170	175
7	198	200
8	226	225
9	255	250
10	283	275
11	311	300
12	340	350
13	368	375
14	396	400
15	428	425
16	456	450

OVEN TEMPERATURE GUIDE

	Electricity		Gas Mark
	°C	°F	
Very cool	110	225	$\frac{1}{4}$
	130	250	$\frac{1}{2}$
Cool	140	275	1
	150	300	2
Moderate	170	325	3
	180	350	4
Moderately hot	190	375	5
	200	400	6
Hot	220	425	7
	230	450	8
Very hot	240	475	9

When using this chart for weights over 16 ounces, add the appropriate figures in the column giving the nearest whole number of grammes and then adjust to the nearest unit of 25. For example, 18 oz (16oz + 2 oz) becomes 456 + 57 = 513 to the nearest whole number and 500 gm to the nearest unit of 25.

Throughout the book, 1 teaspoon = 5 ml and 1 tablespoon = 15 ml.

THE BEGINNING OF COFFEE

Stories of the monastery where the monks did not sleep spread quickly. Kaldi, an Arabian goat herd in Ethiopia, had noticed that his goats were very lively and skittish after they had eaten the lush, red berries that grew on the local bushes. He told the abbot of the nearby monastery who boiled the berries in water and found that the drink helped the monks to stay awake during the long evening prayers.

This is legend but the discovery of coffee growing wild led to its commercial cultivation in the Yemen district of Arabia. Mohammed forbade the drinking of alcohol and coffee became a fragrant substitute, the wine of Araby. By the middle of the sixteenth century, coffee had spread along the caravan trade routes to Egypt, Syria, Greece and Turkey. The many coffee houses in Turkey were visited by the aristocracy and intelligentsia while in the market places, coffee pedlars carried coffee pots heated by spirit lamps. When the Turkish army invaded Western Europe in the seventeenth century, they took this coffee with them. The Turkish army was eventually defeated, but the delicate flavour of the aromatic coffee bean conquered the palates of Europe.

The first coffee house in Britain was opened in 1650 at Oxford. 50 years later, there were some 2,000 coffee houses in London. Stockbrokers met in the warm convivial atmosphere of Jonathan's Coffee House in Change Alley and this became the birthplace of the Stock Exchange. Ship-owners and insurance brokers met at Edward Lloyd's Coffee House in Lombard Street and from this grew Lloyd's of London, now the centre of the world's insurance business. The charge to enter a coffee house was one penny and as places where men exchanged ideas and information, they became known as penny universities.

Coffee trees grow at an altitude of 600 - 2,000 metres between the Tropics of Cancer and Capricorn. The seedlings are transplanted at 6 - 8 months and are planted out at 18 months. There are three main species, the arabica, robusta and liberica. The arabica grows at the highest altitudes and yields the finest berries. The trees are evergreens which will grow to over 6 metres but are usually pruned to 2 metres to make picking easier. The laurel-like leaves grow in pairs opposite each other and the small, white, fragrant flowers last only a few days before giving way to dark green berries. These ripen to golden brown and finally to a rich, dark red. The berries are like cherries, with a golden fleshy layer surrounding two beans lying with their flat surfaces together. Sometimes there is only one seed and this is called a pea-berry. The seeds are covered by an inner husk or parchment and beneath this is a silver skin. The coffee bean is tough, hard and bluish green.

A coffee tree will bear fruit after 3 to 5 years and produce full crops for up to 15 years. Some trees over 100 years old continue to bear fruit. When there is abundant rainfall, a tree may have flowers and cherries at different stages of ripening so that coffee may be picked at all times during the year. The beans are picked by hand and over 4,000 cherries are needed to produce 1 kg of roasted coffee: a skilled picker may reap 90 kg of fruit in a day, yielding 13.5 kg clean coffee ready for roasting.

The beans are processed by a dry or a wet method. In the dry method, the berries are allowed to remain on the trees until they dry out and fall or are shaken on to cloth spread on the ground. The dried pulp, parchment and skin are then removed in one operation.

Higher grades of coffee are obtained by the wet method. A machine, a pulper, removes the soft flesh and the coffee beans are then soaked in water to loosen their outer thin covering. The beans are dried in the sun and then passed through a hulling machine which removes the parchment and silver skin. The green beans are sorted and packed in 60 kg bags.

The flavour of a coffee bean depends on the species and the place where it grows. Different beans are skilfully blended to give the required taste and smell. The beans are roasted and then ground. It is best to grind the beans just before the coffee is used. Manufacturers seal the ground coffee immediately in air tight containers. Instant or soluble coffee is sold as granules or powder.

Instant coffee is 100 per cent pure coffee. Super-heated water is pumped through enormous stainless steel percolators and a dark, strong coffee solution drawn off. This is cooled and sprayed into a tower to meet an upward stream of hot air. The water evaporates leaving fine grains of coffee. These may be combined into larger granules. Freeze-drying is used for the more expensive arabica beans. The percolated coffee is frozen and then subjected to a high vacuum when the frozen water vaporises leaving the coffee frozen. This method gives a better flavour.

The world's largest producer of coffee is Brazil with Columbia second and the Ivory Coast third. The USA buys over a third of the world's coffee.

MORNING COFFEE

For a medium strength coffee, allow 1 teaspoon per cup.

In a saucepan: Warm 40 gm (1 ½ oz) medium or coarsely ground coffee with 500 ml (1 pint) water in a saucepan. Do not boil, and leave over a low heat for 5 minutes. Strain into a warm jug.

In a jug: Place 40 gm (1 ½ oz) medium or coarsely ground coffee in a warm jug and pour 500 ml (1 pint) boiling water over the coffee. Stir, cover and allow to stand for 5 minutes. Strain into another warm jug to serve.

Cona method: This uses a cona or syphon-type coffee maker. Allow 40 gm (1 ½ oz) per 500 ml (1 pint) water. The water is heated in the bottom container and the filter with the coffee is placed in the neck of the top container. When the water boils, steam forces the water through the filter and coffee into the top container. Leave to infuse for 3 minutes and then remove from the heat. The coffee liquid now passes through the filter to the bottom container from which it is served.

Filter method: Place the filter funnel and filter in the neck of a warmed jug. Place 5 tablespoons of ground coffee in the filter and pour over 500 ml (1 pint) boiling water. When filtration is complete, remove the filter funnel and serve the coffee from the jug. Electric filter coffee pots have a thermostat which keeps the coffee at a suitable temperature.

Percolator method: Place 40 gm (1 ½ oz) medium or coarsely ground coffee into the metal basket or filter and 500 ml (1 pint) water in the percolator. Heat

1703

1790

until the water is forced up the central tube and returns through the coffee. The water should percolate for 10 minutes. Electric percolators have a time switch and thermostat.

Expresso method: Place 4 tablespoons coffee in the container and water in the machine. When heated, steam is forced through the coffee and then condenses in a jug.

Instant coffee: This form of coffee has improved greatly and is now very popular. There are many kinds available. Place 1 teaspoon coffee in each cup and fill with boiling water or hot milk and water.

Decaffeinated coffee: Coffee from which caffeine has been removed.

Cappuccino coffee: Italian version of *café au lait*. It is made of a third of a cup of expresso coffee filled with aerated milk and with a light dusting of cinnamon or powdered drinking chocolate.

French coffee: This is ground coffee to which 25 gm (1 oz) chicory is added to 225 gm (8 oz) coffee.

Irish coffee: Pour 3 tablespoons Irish whiskey (or Scotch whisky) into a warm glass. Two-thirds fill the glass with hot, strong coffee, sweeten with brown sugar if preferred, and float thick cream on top.

Italian coffee: Make as for Irish coffee using 3 tablespoons dark rum instead of whisky.

1848

1906

8

Russian coffee: Make as for Irish coffee using 3 tablespoons vodka instead of whisky.

Liqueur coffee: Make as for Irish coffee using liqueurs to taste.

Cointreau coffee: Make as for Irish coffee using Cointreau to taste.

German coffee: Make as for Irish coffee using Kirsch to taste.

Normandy coffee: Make as for Irish coffee using calvados to taste.

Calypso coffee: Make as for Irish coffee using Tia Maria to taste.

Witch's coffee: Make as for Irish coffee using Strega to taste and with a little grated lemon rind sprinkled on top.

Curaçao coffee: Make as for Irish coffee using curaçao to taste and a stick of cinnamon.

Turkish coffee: Place 3 tablespoons finely ground coffee, 1 tablespoon sugar and 125 ml (¼ pint) water in a small deep saucepan and heat until the liquid rises up. Remove from the heat and allow the coffee to sink. Repeat twice but do not allow the coffee to boil. Pour into a small cup and serve with iced water.

Viennese coffee (iced coffee): Cold black coffee, sweetened if preferred, poured into a tall glass and topped with lightly whipped cream *or* cold black coffee poured over ice-cubes in a tall glass and topped with whipped cream *or* cold black coffee to which is added a scoop of vanilla ice cream topped with whipped cream.

Coffee à la brûlot:

1 orange
2 sticks cinnamon, 5 cm (2 inches) long
4 cloves
3 lumps sugar
125 ml (¼ pint) Cognac
500 ml (1 pint) strong black coffee

Pare off the coloured part of the orange skin in one long piece. Place the rind, cinnamon, cloves and sugar in a saucepan. Warm and add the Cognac. Flame and while still burning add the coffee. Ladle into coffee cups.

Coffee milk shake:

125 ml (¼ pint) milk
125 ml (¼ pint) black coffee
1 scoop ice cream

Mix all the ingredients together and whisk.

GINGERBREAD

METRIC	IMPERIAL
450 gm flour	1 lb flour
225 gm demerara sugar	8 oz demerara sugar
150 gm margarine	6 oz margarine
150 gm black treacle	6 oz black treacle
150 gm golden syrup	6 oz golden syrup
225 ml milk	½ pint milk
1 tablespoon ground ginger	1 tablespoon ground ginger
1 tablespoon baking powder	1 tablespoon baking powder
1 tablespoon bicarbonate of soda	1 tablespoon bicarbonate of soda
1 teaspoon salt	1 teaspoon salt
1 egg	1 egg

Sift the flour, baking powder, bicarbonate of soda, ginger and salt together. Place the sugar, margarine, treacle and syrup in a saucepan and heat gently (do not allow to boil) until the fat melts and the ingredients are thoroughly mixed. Leave to cool slightly and add the milk and egg. Make a well in the middle of the dry ingredients and add the liquid. Mix well. Grease and line a 23 cm (9 inch) square cake tin. Place the mixture in the tin and level out. Bake in a moderate oven (170°C, 325°F, gas mark 3) for 1¼ hours until firm to the touch.

SHORTBREAD

METRIC	IMPERIAL
500 gm flour	1 lb flour
250 gm butter	8 oz butter
125 gm caster sugar	4 oz caster sugar

Mix the flour and sugar together and rub the butter into the mixture. Divide into two. Knead lightly into two flat rounds about 0.5 cm (¼ inch) thick. Prick all over with a fork and shape the edge. Mark each into four and bake in a moderate oven (180°C, 350°F, gas mark 4) for 20 minutes.

MACAROONS

METRIC	IMPERIAL
90 gm caster sugar	3½ oz caster sugar
50 gm ground almonds	2 oz ground almonds
¼ teaspoon almond essence	¼ teaspoon almond essence
2 egg whites	2 egg whites
split almonds	split almonds
rice paper	rice paper

Whisk 1 egg white until it is stiff. Fold in the caster sugar, ground almonds and almond essence. Place tablespoonfuls of the mixture on sheets of rice paper on a baking sheet leaving room for the mixture to spread. Place a split almond on top of each biscuit and brush with the remaining egg white. Bake in a moderate oven (180°C, 350°F, gas mark 4) for 20 - 25 minutes. Place on a wire tray to cool.

EVERYDAY SCONES

METRIC	IMPERIAL
200 gm self-raising flour	*8 oz self-raising flour*
50 gm butter	*2 oz butter*
1 teaspoon baking powder	*1 teaspoon baking powder*
¼ teaspoon salt	*¼ teaspoon salt*
125 ml milk	*¼ pint milk*
1 egg	*1 egg*

Sift the flour, baking powder and salt together. Rub in the butter so that the mixture looks like breadcrumbs. Make a well in the centre and pour in the milk to make a fairly soft dough. Turn on to a floured board, knead lightly and roll out to a thickness of 2 cm (¾ inch). Cut into 5 cm (2 inch) rounds and place on a lightly greased baking tin. Lightly beat the egg and brush the scones with the egg. Bake in a hot oven (230°C, 450°F, gas mark 8) for 10 minutes until brown and well risen. Place on a wire tray to cool and serve split and buttered with strawberry jam and whipped cream.

FRUIT SCONES

Make as for everyday scones but stir 50 gm (2 oz) of a mixture of currants and sultanas into the scone mixture after the butter has been rubbed in.

NB Instead of self-raising flour the following may be used:
1 tablespoon bicarbonate of soda for each 200 gm (8 oz plain flour). Sift together twice.

1 teaspoon cream of tartar and ½ teaspoon bicarbonate of soda for each 200 gm (8 oz plain flour) with milk.

½ teaspoon cream of tartar and ¼ teaspoon bicarbonate of soda for each 200 gm (8 oz plain flour) with soured milk.

COUNTRY SCONES

METRIC
200 gm self-raising flour
50 gm butter
50 gm dried mixed fruit
2 tablespoons caster sugar
1 teaspoon baking powder
¼ teaspoon salt
5 tablespoons milk
1 egg

IMPERIAL
8 oz self-raising flour
2 oz butter
2 oz dried mixed fruit
2 tablespoons caster sugar
1 teaspoon baking powder
¼ teaspoon salt
5 tablespoons milk
1 egg

Sift the flour, salt and baking powder together. Rub in the butter until the mixture looks like breadcrumbs. Stir in the fruit and sugar. Lightly beat the egg and add with the milk to make a fairly soft dough. Turn on to a floured board and knead lightly. Roll out to a thickness of 2 cm (¾ inch) and cut into 5 cm (2 inch) rounds. Place on a lightly greased baking sheet and brush with milk. Bake in a hot oven (230°C, 450°F, gas mark 8) for 10 minutes until brown and well risen. Place on a wire tray to cool. Serve split and buttered with strawberry jam and whipped cream.

WHOLEWHEAT SCONES

Replace 100 gm (4 oz) flour in the recipe for country scones by 100 gm (4 oz) wholewheat flour.

CHERRY SCONES

Omit the fruit from the recipe for country scones. Roll out the dough and cut into rounds. Using a smaller cutter, remove the centres from half the rounds. Place the rings formed on the other rounds. Brush with milk and place a teaspoon of cherry jam in the centre of each. Bake in a hot oven (230°C, 450°F, gas mark 8) for 10 minutes until brown and well risen. Place on a wire tray to cool. (Use other jams if preferred.)

CHEESE SCONES

METRIC	IMPERIAL
200 gm self-raising flour	*8 oz self-raising flour*
25 gm butter	*1 oz butter*
50 gm Cheddar cheese	*2 oz Cheddar cheese*
1 teaspoon baking powder	*1 teaspoon baking powder*
¼ teaspoon dry mustard	*¼ teaspoon dry mustard*
125 ml milk	*¼ pint milk*
pinch of salt	*pinch of salt*

Sift the flour, baking powder and salt together. Rub in the butter until the mixture looks like breadcrumbs. Grate the cheese. Stir in the cheese and dry mustard. Add enough milk to form a fairly soft dough. Turn on to a floured board and roll out to a thickness of 2 cm (¾ inches). Cut into 5 cm (2 inch) rounds and place on a lightly greased baking dish. Brush with milk or sprinkle with a little more grated cheese. Bake in a hot oven (220°C, 425°F, gas mark 7) for 10 minutes. Place on a wire tray to cool. Serve split and buttered.

DROP SCONES

METRIC	IMPERIAL
200 gm self-raising flour	8 oz self-raising flour
50 gm butter	2 oz butter
50 gm caster sugar	2 oz caster sugar
125 ml milk	¼ pint milk
125 ml water	¼ pint water
1 egg	1 egg
pinch of salt	pinch of salt

Sift the flour and salt together. Rub in the butter until the mixture looks like breadcrumbs. Stir in the caster sugar. Break the egg into a cup and pour into the centre of the mixture. Mix the milk and water and add a little to the egg. Stir the mixture and beat well. Slowly add the remaining liquid, beating well to keep the mixture smooth. Leave to stand for 15 minutes. Drop the batter, 2 tablespoonfuls at a time on to a very hot greased griddle. Cook until the mixture bubbles on the surface. Turn and cook on the other side. Serve warm and buttered with jam.

GRIDDLE CAKES

METRIC	IMPERIAL
200 gm self-raising flour	8 oz gm self-raising flour
100 gm butter	4 oz butter
75 gm caster sugar	3 oz caster sugar
50 gm currants	2 oz currants
1 teaspoon baking powder	1 teaspoon baking powder
¼ teaspoon mixed spice	¼ teaspoon mixed spice

METRIC	IMPERIAL
2 tablespoons milk	2 tablespoons milk
1 egg	1 egg
pinch of salt	pinch of salt

Sift the flour, baking powder, salt and mixed spice together. Rub in the butter until the mixture looks like breadcrumbs. Stir in the sugar and fruit. Lightly beat the egg and add with the milk to form a firm dough. Roll out on a floured board to a thickness of 1.5 cm (⅛ inch) and cut into 5 cm (2 inch) rounds. Cook on a greased griddle over a gentle heat allowing 3 minutes on each side. Cool on a wire tray and sprinkle with caster sugar. Serve alone or buttered. (The griddle should be rubbed with salt and then thoroughly wiped with kitchen paper. Heat slowly for 15 minutes and grease lightly before using. A thick frying pan may be used instead of a griddle or girdle).

RASPBERRY POPOVERS

METRIC	IMPERIAL
100 gm plain flour	4 oz plain flour
200 ml milk	⅓ pint milk
2 eggs	2 eggs
pinch of salt	pinch of salt
raspberry jam	raspberry jam

Sift the flour and salt. Beat the eggs. Add the eggs and milk slowly to the flour, beating to make a smooth batter. Leave to stand for 30 minutes. Half fill greased bun tins and bake in a hot oven (220 °C, 425°F, gas mark 7) for 15 - 20 minutes until crisp with a thin golden brown crust. A few minutes before baking is complete, puncture the popovers with a fork. This allows the insides to dry a little. When cooked, split and fill with raspberry jam. Serve immediately.

FRUIT LOAF

METRIC	IMPERIAL
200 gm self raising flour	*8 oz self raising flour*
100 gm margarine	*4 oz margarine*
100 gm caster sugar	*4 oz caster sugar*
50 gm currants	*2 oz currants*
50 gm sultanas	*2 oz sultanas*
50 gm cherries	*2 oz cherries*
grated rind of 1 lemon	*grated rind of 1 lemon*
1 egg	*1 egg*
4 -5 tablespoons milk	*4 - 5 tablespoons milk*
pinch of salt	*pinch of salt*

Sift the flour and salt together. Rub in the margarine until the mixture looks like breadcrumbs. Add the fruit and lemon rind. Mix well. Mix the egg with 4 tablespoons milk and add to the mixture. Add a little more milk if necessary so that the mixture is firm but will just drop from a spoon if gently shaken. Grease and line a 15 cm (6 inch) cake tin. Turn the mixture into the tin and cook in a moderate oven (180 °C, 350°F, gas mark 4) for 1 - 1 ½ hours until firm. Cook and serve sliced and buttered.

TEACAKES

METRIC
300 gm plain flour
25 gm lard
15 gm fresh yeast or
  2 teaspoons dried yeast and
  1 teaspoon caster sugar
75 gm currants and sultanas mixed
170 ml tepid milk and water mixed
1 egg
pinch of salt

IMPERIAL
12 oz gm plain flour
1 oz lard
½ oz fresh yeast or
  2 teaspoons dried yeast and
  1 teaspoon caster sugar
3 oz currants and sultanas mixed
⅓ pint tepid milk and water mixed
1 egg
pinch of salt

Cream the yeast with a little of the milk and then add the rest of the milk or dissolve the sugar in the milk and sprinkle the dried yeast on top and leave to stand for a few minutes until frothy. Make a well in the middle of the flour and stir in the yeast liquid. Lightly beat the egg and add to the dough. Warm the lard and knead into the mixture. Knead lightly until smooth. Cover and leave in a warm place until the dough has doubled in size. Knead the salt and fruit into the dough. Divide into 10 pieces and flatten into rounds. Place, well apart, on a greased baking sheet. Cover, and leave in a warm place for 15 minutes until well risen. Bake in a hot oven (230°C, 450°F, gas mark 8) for 15 minutes. Cool on a wire tray. Serve split and buttered or split, toasted, buttered and warm.

WHOLEWHEAT BUNS

METRIC	IMPERIAL
25 gm fresh yeast or	*1 oz fresh yeast or*
15 gm dried yeast and	*½ oz dried yeast and*
1 teaspoon sugar	*1 teaspoon sugar*
125 ml tepid water	*¼ pint tepid water*
450 gm wholewheat flour	*1 lb wholewheat flour*
40 gm dark brown sugar	*1½ oz dark brown sugar*
1 teaspoon mixed spice	*1 teaspoon mixed spice*
¼ teaspoon ground cinnamon	*¼ teaspoon ground cinnamon*
dusting of nutmeg	*dusting of nutmeg*
pinch of salt	*pinch of salt*
50 gm margarine	*2 oz margarine*
100 gm mixed fruit	*4 oz mixed fruit*
(currants, sultanas, peel)	*(currants, sultanas, peel)*
1 egg	*1 egg*
milk	*milk*
Glaze	***Glaze***
1 tablespoon demerara sugar	*1 tablespoon demerara sugar*
2 tablespoons water	*2 tablespoons water*

Mix the fresh yeast with 1 teaspoon sugar and stir into the tepid water. If using dried yeast, add the teaspoon of sugar to the tepid water and sprinkle the yeast on top. Stir into the water. Leave to stand in a warm place for 10 - 15 minutes. Sift the flour, salt and spices together. Rub in the margarine until the mixture looks like breadcrumbs. Add the sugar and fruit. Mix well. Beat the egg and add enough warm milk to make 125 ml (a scant ¼ pint). Add the yeast liquid and egg and milk to the dry ingredients and mix. Knead thoroughly. Cover with a cloth and leave to stand in a warm

20

place for 1 hour until the dough has doubled in size. Turn on to a floured board and knead well. Divide into 8 pieces and shape into buns. Place on a greased baking tray, cover and leave to rise in a warm place for a further hour. Bake in a moderately hot oven (200°C, 400°F, gas mark 6) for 15 minutes until brown. Brush with glaze while hot. **Glaze:** Dissolve the sugar in the water over a low heat and boil until syrupy.

FRUIT BUNS

METRIC	IMPERIAL
200 gm self raising flour	*8 oz self raising flour*
100 gm margarine	*4 oz margarine*
75 gm caster sugar	*3 oz caster sugar*
50 gm currants	*2 oz currants*
pinch salt	*pinch salt*
1 egg	*1 egg*
2 tablespoons milk	*2 tablespoons milk*

Sift the flour and salt together. Rub in the margarine until the mixture looks like breadcrumbs. Add the sugar and fruit. Lightly beat the egg and add the milk. Add enough liquid to the bun mixture to make a stiff consistency. Place heaped tablespoons of the mixture on a greased baking tin, leaving enough space for each to rise. Cook in hot oven (220°C, 425°F, gas mark 7) for 12 - 15 minutes.

ASSORTED CAKES

METRIC	IMPERIAL
100 gm self-raising flour	*4 oz self-raising flour*
100 gm butter	*4 oz butter*
100 gm caster sugar	*4 oz caster sugar*
2 eggs	*2 eggs*

Cream the butter and sugar until creamy and fluffy. Slowly beat in the eggs one at a time. Sift the flour and fold into the cake mixture. Place paper cases in a patty cake tin and two-thirds fill each case with the mixture. Bake in a moderate oven (180 °C, 350 °F, gas mark 4) for 15 minutes. Cool on a wire tray. Decorate with white or chocolate glacé icing or piped butter icing or whipped cream.

CHOCOLATE ASSORTED CAKES

Sift 1 tablespoon powdered drinking chocolate with the flour in the above recipe.

CHOCOLATE CAKE

METRIC	IMPERIAL
100 gm butter	*4 oz butter*
100 gm caster sugar	*4 oz caster sugar*
100 gm flour	*4 oz flour*
3 tablespoons cocoa	*3 tablespoons cocoa*
1 tablespoon water	*1 tablespoon water*
2 eggs	*2 eggs*
chocolate butter cream	*chocolate butter cream*

Cream the butter and sugar together until pale and creamy. Add the eggs, one at a time, beating well after each has been added. Dissolve the cocoa in the water and beat into the creamed mixture. Fold in the flour using a metal spoon. Divide the mixture between two greased 18 cm (7 inch) sandwich tins. Level off the mixture in the tins with the flat side of a knife. Bake in a moderately hot oven (190°C, 375°F, gas mark 5) for 20 minutes until firm to the touch. Turn on to a wire tray to cool. Sandwich together with chocolate butter cream or whipped fresh cream. Serve slices with whipped fresh cream.

CHOCOLATE BUTTER CREAM

METRIC	IMPERIAL
75 gm butter	*3 oz butter*
150 gm icing sugar	*6 oz icing sugar*
9 teaspoons water	*9 teaspoons water*
1 tablespoon cocoa	*1 tablespoon cocoa*

Sift the icing sugar. Cream the butter until it is soft. Add the sugar and cream until the mixture is smooth. Dissolve the cocoa in a little of the water. Add the cocoa and remaining water to the icing. Beat well.

CHOCOLATE SPICE CAKE

METRIC	IMPERIAL
50 gm plain chocolate	2 oz plain chocolate
3 tablespoons cocoa	3 tablespoons cocoa
75 gm plain white flour	3 oz plain white flour
75 gm plain wholemeal flour	3 oz plain wholemeal flour
2 teaspoons baking powder	2 teaspoons baking powder
2 teaspoons mixed spice	2 teaspoons mixed spice
175 gm caster sugar	6 oz caster sugar
225 gm soft margarine	8 oz soft margarine
3 eggs	3 eggs
4 tablespoons milk	4 tablespoons milk
Icing	*Icing*
200 gm icing sugar	8 oz icing sugar
2 tablespoons cocoa	2 tablespoons cocoa
75 gm soft margarine	3 oz soft margarine
75 gm caster sugar	3 oz caster sugar
3 tablespoons milk	3 tablespoons milk

Cake: Break the chocolate into pieces into a bowl standing over a pan of hot water. Add the cocoa and milk. Stir until smooth and leave to cool. Place the flours, baking powder, spice, caster sugar and soft margarine in a bowl. Lightly beat the eggs and add with the chocolate liquid to the flour mixture. Whisk well until thoroughly mixed and smooth. Grease and line a 25 x 18 cm (10 x 7 inch) baking tin. Turn the cake mixture into the tin and bake in a moderate oven (180°C, 350°F, gas mark 4) for 50 minutes until firm to the touch.

Icing: Sieve the icing sugar and cocoa powder together. Heat the margarine, caster sugar and milk until the sugar dissolves. Bring to the boil. Add the icing sugar and cocoa and beat until the mixture thickens. Spread over the cake. Leave to cool before serving.

COCONUT CAKE

METRIC	IMPERIAL
200 gm self-raising flour	8 oz self-raising flour
125 gm margarine	5 oz margarine
125 oz caster sugar	5 oz caster sugar
100 gm desiccated coconut	4 oz desiccated cocoanut
3 eggs	3 eggs
3 tablespoons milk	3 tablespoons milk
pinch of salt	pinch of salt
Icing	*Icing*
150 gm icing sugar	6 oz icing sugar
50 gm butter	2 oz butter
50 gm desiccated coconut	2 oz desiccated coconut

Cake: Cream the margarine and sugar. Beat in the eggs one at a time. Sift the flour and salt together and mix with the coconut. Fold the coconut mixture into the creamed mixture alternately adding the milk. Turn into a greased, lined 18 cm (7 inch) cake tin and bake in a moderate oven (180°C, 350°F, gas mark 4) for 1 - 1¼ hours until firm. Turn out onto a wire tray to cool.

Icing: Sift the icing sugar and cream with the butter. Coat the cake with the icing and cover with coconut.

MADEIRA CAKE

METRIC	IMPERIAL
100 gm self-raising flour	*4 oz self-raising flour*
100 gm plain four	*4 oz plain four*
150 gm butter	*6 oz butter*
150 gm caster sugar	*6 oz caster sugar*
1 teaspoon vanilla essence	*1 teaspoon vanilla essence*
2 tablespoons milk	*2 tablespoons milk*
3 eggs	*3 eggs*
3 slices of citron peel	*3 slices of citron peel*
pinch of salt	*pinch of salt*

Sift the flours and salt together. Cream the butter, sugar and vanilla essence together until creamy and fluffy. Beat in the eggs, one at a time. Fold in the flour with enough milk to give a dropping consistency. Turn into a greased and lined 18 cm (7 inch) cake tin and bake in a moderately oven (180°C, 350°F, gas mark 4) for 1 - 1¼ hours. After 20 minutes, place the citron peel across the top of the cake.

CHERRY CAKE

Stir 100 gm (4 oz) glacé cherries in the recipe for madeira cake. Prepare the cherries by cutting each in half and rolling them in flour.

FRUIT CAKE

Replace the caster sugar in the recipe for madeira cake by 150 gm (6 oz) soft brown sugar and stir 200 gm (8 oz) mixed dried fruit and 50 gm (2 oz) mixed peel into the cake mixture. Cover the top with blanched split almonds.

FARMHOUSE CAKE

METRIC	IMPERIAL
200 gm plain flour	8 oz plain flour
200 gm wholemeal flour	8 oz wholemeal flour
1 teaspoon bicarbonate of soda	1 teaspoon bicarbonate of soda
2 teaspoons mixed spice	2 teaspoons mixed spice
150 gm butter	6 oz butter
200 gm brown sugar	8 oz brown sugar
200 gm mixed dried fruit	8 oz mixed dried fruit
1 egg	1 egg
250 ml milk	½ pint milk

Sift the plain flour, bicarbonate of soda and spice together. Stir in the wholemeal flour. Rub the flour mixture and butter together until the mixture looks like breadcrumbs. Stir in the sugar and fruit. Beat the egg and milk lightly and add to the centre of the dry ingredients. Mix well to give a soft dropping consistency. Turn into a greased, lined 20.5 cm (8 inch) square tin and bake in a moderate oven (170°C, 325°F, gas mark 3) for 1 hour 40 minutes until cooked when tested with a knife. Turn out and leave to cool.

CUSTARD SLICES

METRIC	IMPERIAL
200 gm plain flour	*8 oz plain flour*
150 gm butter	*6 oz butter*
7 tablespoons cold water	*7 tablespoons cold water*
pinch of salt	*pinch of salt*
½ teaspoon lemon juice	*½ teaspoon lemon juice*

Sift the flour and salt together. Cut the butter into small cubes and stir into the flour. Mix to a firm dough with the water and lemon juice. Turn on to a floured board and roll out to a strip three times as long as it is wide. Fold the top third of the strip down and the bottom third up. Turn the pastry so that the folds are at the sides and roll out again. Repeat until the pastry has been folded four times. Cover and leave to rest for 30 minutes. Roll out thinly and use to line two rectangular Swiss tins. Bake in a hot oven (220°C, 425°F, gas mark 7) for 20 minutes until crisp and well risen. Sandwich with custard and coat with glacé icing. Cut into slices.

CUSTARD

METRIC	IMPERIAL
1 egg white	*1 egg white*
2 egg yolks	*2 egg yolks*
50 gm caster sugar	*2 oz caster sugar*
2 tablespoons plain flour	*2 tablespoons plain flour*
2 tablespoons cornflour	*2 tablespoons cornflour*
250 ml milk	*½ pint milk*
vanilla essence	*vanilla essence*

Beat the egg yolks and sugar until creamy. Beat in the flours and add a little milk to make a smooth paste. Heat the rest of the milk and when nearly boiling stir into the egg mixture. Return the custard to the saucepan and heat slowly with constant stirring until the mixture thickens. Beat the egg white until stiff. Remove the custard from the heat and fold in the egg white. Add a few drops of vanilla essence and re-heat for 2 - 3 minutes. Cool before using.

GLACE ICING

METRIC
150 gm icing sugar
2 tablespoons warm water

IMPERIAL
6 oz icing sugar
2 tablespoons warm water

Sift the sugar and stir in the water to make an icing that is thick enough to coat the back of a spoon.

CREAM SLICES

Make as for custard slices but sandwich together with a little raspberry jam and whipped cream.

CHERRY SLICES

METRIC
100 gm butter
100 gm self-raising flour
100 gm caster sugar
2 eggs
Filling
whipped cream
50 gm glacé cherries

IMPERIAL
4 oz butter
4 oz self-raising flour
4 oz caster sugar
2 eggs
Filling
whipped cream
2 oz glacé cherries

Cream the butter and sugar together until light and fluffy. Add the eggs, one at a time, beating well after each has been added. Fold in the flour using a metal spoon. Divide between two rectangular sponge tins and level using the flat side of a knife. Bake in a moderately hot oven (190°C, 375°F, gas mark 5) for 15 - 20 minutes. Turn on to a wire tray to cool. Cut the glacé cherries in half and mix with the cream. Sandwich the sponges together with the cream mixture and dust with icing sugar. Cut into slices.

STRAWBERRY SLICES

Replace the cherries in the recipe for cherry slices by 100 gm (4 oz) strawberries. Wash and hull the strawberries and cut into pieces.

ECLAIRS

METRIC	IMPERIAL
Choux pastry	*Choux pastry*
50 gm butter	*2 oz butter*
8 tablespoons plain flour	*8 tablespoons plain flour*
125 ml water	*¼ pint water*
2 eggs	*2 eggs*
125 ml double cream	*¼ pint double cream*
chocolate glacé icing	*chocolate glacé icing*

Warm the butter in the water in a saucepan until it melts. Sift the flour. Remove the saucepan from the heat and add all the flour all at once. Beat with a wooden spoon to a smooth paste. Warm the pastry a little until it comes away from the sides of the pan. Allow to cool slightly. Add the eggs, a little at a time, beating vigorously until a mixture of piping consistency is formed. (An electric beater is best.) Pipe the choux pastry into 9 cm (3 ½ inch) strips using a piping bag fitted with a plain nozzle of 1.25 cm (½ inch) diameter. Bake in a moderately hot oven (200°C, 400°F, gas mark 6) for 35 minutes. Cut the éclairs open to dry. Before serving, fill with whipped cream and coat with chocolate glacé icing.

CHOCOLATE GLACE ICING

METRIC	IMPERIAL
150 gm icing sugar	*6 oz gm icing sugar*
2 tablespoons warm water	*2 tablespoons warm water*
50 gm chocolate	*2 oz chocolate*

Sift the icing sugar and melt the chocolate. Stir the warm water and melted chocolate into the sugar.

PROFITEROLES

METRIC
choux pastry
125 ml double cream
icing sugar
chocolate sauce

IMPERIAL
choux pastry
¼ pint double cream
icing sugar
chocolate sauce

Make choux pastry as in the recipe for éclairs. Pipe the pastry into small balls 4 cm (1.5 inches) across on a wet baking sheet using a piping bag with a 1.25 cm (½ inch) plain nozzle. Bake in a hot oven (220°C, 425°F, gas mark 7) for 20 minutes. When cool, make a small hole in the bottom of each and fill with whipped cream. Pile on a plate and dust with icing sugar. Pour over the chocolate sauce before serving.

CHOCOLATE SAUCE

METRIC
50 gm plain chocolate
1 tablespoon milk
1 teaspoon vanilla essence
knob of butter

IMPERIAL
2 oz plain chocolate
1 tablespoon milk
1 teaspoon vanilla essence
knob of butter

Melt the chocolate and butter in a basin over hot water. Stir in the milk and vanilla essence. Stir and pour over the profiteroles just before serving.

COCONUT TARTS

METRIC
The pastry
50 gm butter
100 gm plain flour
1 teaspoon caster sugar
1 egg yolk
pinch of salt
Filling
50 gm butter
50 gm caster sugar
50 gm desiccated coconut
3 tablespoons self-raising flour
1 egg
raspberry jam

IMPERIAL
The pastry
2 oz butter
4 oz plain flour
1 teaspoon caster sugar
1 egg yolk
pinch of salt
Filling
2 oz butter
2 oz caster sugar
2 oz desiccated coconut
3 tablespoons self-raising flour
1 egg
raspberry jam

The pastry: Sift the flour and salt together and rub in the butter until the mixture looks like breadcrumbs. Stir in the sugar. Make a well in the middle and add the egg yolk with enough water to make a stiff dough. Turn on to a floured board, knead lightly and roll out. Cut into 6 cm (2½ inch) rounds and use to line 18 greased patty tins.
Filling: Cream the butter and sugar until light and fluffy. Add the egg and beat well. Fold in the flour and coconut using a metal spoon. Place a teaspoonful of raspberry jam in each pastry case and then nearly fill each with the coconut mixture. Bake in a moderately hot oven (190ºC, 375ºF, gas mark 5) for 15 - 20 minutes. Cool on a wire rack.

JAM TARTS

METRIC	IMPERIAL
200 gm plain flour	*8 oz plain flour*
100 gm butter	*4 oz butter*
9 teaspoons water	*9 teaspoons water*
pinch of salt	*pinch of salt*
raspberry jam	*raspberry jam*

Sift the salt and flour together. Rub in the butter until the mixture looks like breadcrumbs. Stir in the water and form the mixture into a firm dough. Roll out on a floured board and cut into 7.5 cm (3 inch) rounds. Line patty tins with the pastry and two-thirds fill with raspberry jam. Bake in a hot oven (220ºC, 425ºF, gas mark 7) for 15 minutes.

STRAWBERRY BOATS

METRIC	IMPERIAL
pastry as for jam tarts above	*pastry as for jam tarts above*
strawberry jam	*strawberry jam*
whipped cream	*whipped cream*
fresh strawberries	*fresh strawberries*
4 tablespoons raspberry jelly	*4 tablespoons raspberry jelly*

Roll out the pastry and use to line 16 boat shaped tins. Prick all over and bake in a hot oven (220ºC, 425ºF, gas mark 7) for 10 - 5 minutes. Carefully turn out and leave to cool. (These may be made beforehand and stored in an airtight tin.) Line with jam and cream and fill with strawberries. Heat the jelly in a bowl over hot water until the jelly melts. Allow to cool slightly until it becomes sticky and use to coat the strawberries.

SAVOURY SAUSAGE ROLLS

METRIC
200 gm plain flour
75 gm margarine
75 gm grated Cheddar cheese
1 egg yolk
¼ teaspoon salt
¼ teaspoon dry mustard
pinch cayenne pepper
2 tablespoons water
Filling
200 gm sausage meat
1 large onion
fat for frying

IMPERIAL
8 oz plain flour
3 oz margarine
3 oz Cheddar cheese
1 egg yolk
¼ teaspoon salt
¼ teaspoon dry mustard
pinch cayenne pepper
2 tablespoons water
Filling
8 oz sausage meat
1 large onion
fat for frying

Sift the flour, salt, mustard and pepper together. Rub in the margarine until the mixture looks like breadcrumbs. Stir in the cheese. Add the egg yolk and water to form a firm dough. Knead lightly then roll out thinly. Skin and chop the onion. Fry gently until softened. Mix with the sausage meat and form into a long sausage. Cover the sausage mixture with pastry and cut into 5 cm (2 inch pieces). Repeat until all the meat is used up. Bake on a baking sheet in a fairly hot oven (200°C, 400°F, gas mark 6) for 15 minutes and then in a moderate oven (180°C, 350°F, gas mark 4) for a further 15 minutes.

VIENNESE BISCUITS

METRIC
150 gm flour
150 gm butter
50 gm caster sugar
chocolate

IMPERIAL
6 oz flour
6 oz butter
2 oz caster sugar
chocolate

Cream the butter and sugar until soft and fluffy. Work in the flour. Using a fluted nozzle and forcing bag, pipe fingers of the mixture 6 cm (2½ inches) long on to a greased baking tray. Cook in a moderate oven (180°C, 350°F, gas mark 4) for 10 minutes until firm but only slightly coloured. Melt the chocolate in a basin over hot water and dip the ends of the biscuits in it.

CHOCOLATE BROWNIES

METRIC
75 gm plain flour
75 gm margarine
50 gm plain cooking chocolate
150 gm caster sugar
50 gm chopped walnuts
1 teaspoon vanilla essence
¼ teaspoon baking powder
pinch of salt
2 eggs

IMPERIAL
3 oz plain flour
3 oz margarine
2 oz plain cooking chocolate
6 oz caster sugar
2 oz chopped walnuts
1 teaspoon vanilla essence
¼ teaspoon baking powder
pinch of salt
2 eggs

Melt the chocolate with the margarine in a large basin standing over hot water. Allow to cool slightly. Beat the eggs. Stir the eggs, sugar, vanilla essence and walnuts into the melted chocolate. Mix. Sift the flour, salt and baking powder together and fold into the chocolate mixture. Pour into a greased, lined shallow 18 cm (7 inch) tin and bake in a moderate oven (180ºC, 350ºF, gas mark 4) for 40 minutes until firm. Leave to cool in the tin. Sprinkle with caster sugar while still warm. When cool, turn out and cut into slices.

CHOCOLATE BISCUITS

METRIC	IMPERIAL
100 gm margarine	*4 oz margarine*
100 gm caster sugar	*4 oz caster sugar*
200 gm flour	*8 oz flour*
1 teaspoon baking powder	*1 teaspoon baking powder*
pinch cinnamon	*pinch cinnamon*
50 gm cocoa or chocolate powder	*2 oz cocoa or chocolate powder*
1 egg	*1 egg*

Cream the margarine and sugar. Lightly beat the egg and beat into the mixture. Sieve the flour, baking powder, cinnamon and cocoa or chocolate powder together. Fold into the mixture. Leave to stand in a cool place for 15 minutes.

Roll out to a thickness of 0.5 cm (¼ inch) and cut into 5 cm (2 inch) rounds. Bake on a greased baking sheet in a moderate oven (180ºC, 350ºF, gas mark 4) for 10 - 15 minutes. When cool, serve plain or iced.

CHOCOLATE DROPS

METRIC	IMPERIAL
100 gm caster sugar	*4 oz caster sugar*
100 gm chocolate powder	*4 oz chocolate powder*
3 egg whites	*3 egg whites*
3 drops vanilla essence	*3 drops vanilla essence*

Beat the eggs white until they are stiff. Stir in the sugar, chocolate powder and vanilla essence. Place teaspoonfuls on a greased baking tin and cook in a moderate oven (180°C, 350°F, gas mark 4) for 15 - 20 minutes.

GINGER BISCUITS

METRIC	IMPERIAL
150 gm plain flour	*6 oz plain flour*
75 gm sugar	*3 oz sugar*
75 gm butter	*3 oz butter*
2 teaspoons ground ginger	*2 teaspoons ground ginger*
1 teaspoon salt	*1 teaspoon salt*
1 egg	*1 egg*

Sift the flour, salt and ground ginger together. Rub the butter into the flour so that the mixture looks like breadcrumbs. Stir in the remaining dry ingredients and bind together with egg. Roll out and cut into 5 cm (2 inch) rounds. Bake on a baking tin in a moderately hot oven (190°C, 375°F, gas mark 5) for 15 minutes.

CINNAMON BISCUITS

METRIC	IMPERIAL
75 gm butter	3 oz butter
75 gm caster sugar	3 oz caster sugar
150 gm flour	6 oz flour
1 teaspoon cinnamon	1 teaspoon cinnamon
2 eggs	2 eggs

Cream the sugar and butter. Separate the eggs and beat in the egg yolks, one at a time. Sieve the flour and cinnamon together and add to the butter mixture. Knead lightly until smooth. Roll out thinly on a floured board and cut into 5 cm (2 inch) rounds. Brush lightly with egg white. Bake in a moderate oven (180°C, 350°F, gas mark 4) for 10 - 15 minutes until firm and brown.

NUTTY BISCUITS

METRIC	IMPERIAL
75 gm self-raising flour	3 oz self-raising flour
75 gm butter	3 oz butter
75 gm caster sugar	3 oz caster sugar
25 gm chopped nuts	1 oz chopped nuts
milk to bind	milk to bind

Rub the fat and flour together until the mixture looks like breadcrumbs. Stir in the sugar and chopped nuts. Squeeze together with a little milk if necessary. Roll out thinly and cut into rounds. Bake in a moderate oven (180°C, 350°F, gas mark 4) for 10 - 15 minutes until firm.

LEMON BISCUITS

METRIC	IMPERIAL
150 gm butter	*6 oz butter*
300 gm flour	*12 oz flour*
100 gm caster sugar	*4 oz caster sugar*
1 egg	*1 egg*
1 lemon	*1 lemon*

Squeeze and strain the juice from the lemon. Grate the rind. Rub the fat and flour together until the mixture looks like breadcrumbs. Stir in the sugar and lemon rind. Beat the egg and add with the lemon juice to the flour mixture. Roll out and cut into 5 cm (2 inch) rounds. Bake on a greased baking tin (180°C, 350°F, gas mark 4) for 10 - 15 minutes. Serve plain or iced with lemon curd and lemon icing.

LEMON ICING

METRIC	IMPERIAL
150 gm icing sugar	*6 oz icing sugar*
1 lemon	*1 lemon*

Squeeze and strain the juice from the lemon. Sift the sugar and stir in the juice to make an icing that is thick enough to coat the back of a spoon.

WAFER BISCUITS

METRIC	IMPERIAL
50 gm brown sugar	*2 oz brown sugar*
50 gm butter	*2 oz butter*
2 tablespoons syrup	*2 tablespoons syrup*
150 gm flour	*6 oz flour*
¼ teaspoon ground ginger	*¼ teaspoon ground ginger*
¼ teaspoon baking powder	*¼ teaspoon baking powder*

Melt the sugar, butter and syrup together, taking care not to burn the mixture. Remove from the heat and mix in the remaining ingredients to form a stiff paste. Roll out as thin as possible and cut into rounds. Prick all over and bake in a moderate oven (170°C, 325°F, gas mark 3) until firm and slightly coloured.

COUNTRY BISCUITS

METRIC	IMPERIAL
100 gm butter	*4 oz butter*
75 gm caster sugar	*3 oz caster sugar*
125 gm self-raising flour	*5 oz self-raising flour*
75 gm porridge oats	*3 oz porridge oats*
1 tablespoon cocoa	*1 tablespoon cocoa*
¼ teaspoon vanilla essence	*¼ teaspoon vanilla essence*

Cream the butter and sugar together. Sift the flour and cocoa together and mix into the butter/sugar mixture. Add all the remaining ingredients. Roll into small pieces and place on a greased baking tray. Bake in a cool oven (150°C, 300°F, gas mark 2) for 35 minutes.

OATMEAL BISCUITS

METRIC
150 gm wholewheat flour
25 gm oatmeal
1 teaspoon baking powder
75 gm butter
40 gm soft brown sugar
pinch of salt
2 - 3 tablespoons milk

IMPERIAL
6 oz wholewheat flour
1 oz oatmeal
1 teaspoon baking powder
3 oz butter
1½ oz soft brown sugar
pinch of salt
2 - 3 tablespoons milk

Sift the salt and baking powder together. Mix the flour and oatmeal. Add the salt and baking powder. Rub in the butter until the mixture looks like breadcrumbs. Stir in the sugar. Add enough milk to make a stiff consistency. Roll out to a thickness of ½ cm (¼ inch) on a greased board. Cut into 6 cm (2 ½ inch) rounds. Bake in a moderately hot oven (190 °C, 375ºF, gas mark 5) for 10 - 15 minutes.

WHOLEWHEAT BISCUITS

METRIC
200 gm wholewheat flour
100 gm plain flour
200 gm butter
50 gm caster sugar
pinch salt
1 egg

IMPERIAL
8 oz wholewheat flour
4 oz plain flour
8 oz butter
2 oz caster sugar
pinch salt
1 egg

Sift the flours and salt together. Rub the fat into the flours until the mixture looks like breadcrumbs. Stir in the caster sugar. Beat the egg and add to the flour mixture to form a firm paste. Add a little milk if necessary. Leave to stand for 30 minutes. Roll out on a floured board to a thickness of 1 cm (⅓ inch) and cut into rounds. Prick all over. Bake on a greased baking tin in a moderate oven (180ºC, 350ºF, gas mark 4) for 10 - 15 minutes until firm.

CHEESE BISCUITS

METRIC
100 gm butter
100 gm flour
100 gm grated Parmesan cheese
50 gm grated Cheddar cheese
1 egg yolk or 2 tablespoons milk
salt
cayenne pepper

IMPERIAL
4 oz butter
4 oz flour
4 oz grated Parmesan cheese
2 oz grated Cheddar cheese
1 egg yolk or 2 tablespoons milk
salt
cayenne pepper

Rub the fat into the flour until the mixture looks like breadcrumbs. Stir in the cheese and season with salt and pepper. Bind with the egg yolk and water or with the milk. Roll out thinly on a floured board and cut into rounds. Bake on a greased baking sheet in a hot oven (220ºC, 425ºF, gas mark 7) for 10 - 15 minutes until lightly brown.

CHEESE STRAWS

Make as for the above recipe but roll out and cut into strips.

AMERICAN COOKIES

METRIC	IMPERIAL
150 gm plain flour	*6 oz plain flour*
1 teaspoon baking powder	*1 teaspoon baking powder*
¼ teaspoon salt	*¼ teaspoon salt*
100 gm butter	*4 oz butter*
200 gm caster sugar	*8 oz caster sugar*
1 egg	*1 egg*
3 teaspoons milk	*3 teaspoons milk*
¼ teaspoon vanilla essence	*¼ teaspoon vanilla essence*

Sift the flour, baking powder and salt together. Cream the butter and sugar. Beat in the egg, milk and vanilla essence. Add the flour mixture, a little at a time, and beating all the while. Drop teaspoonfuls 20 cm (2 inches) apart on a lightly greased baking sheet and cook in a moderate oven (180°C, 350°F, gas mark 4) for 8 - 10 minutes until firm.

ROLLED COOKIES

Mix as for above but use 200 gm (8 oz) plain flour to make a firmer mixture. Roll out thinly on a floured board and cut into rounds. Brush with egg white mixed with a teaspoon of water. Cook on a greased baking sheet in a moderate oven (180°C, 350°F, gas mark 4) for 10 - 15 minutes until firm. Dust with sugar before serving.

BUTTERSCOTCH COOKIES

Make as for American Cookies but use brown sugar instead of white and add 25 gm (1 oz) chopped nuts.

CHOCOLATE COOKIES

Sift 25 gm (1 oz) cocoa powder or chocolate powder with the flour mixture in the recipe for American cookies. If chocolate powder is used, use slightly less sugar.

CINNAMON COOKIES

Sieve half a teaspoon each of powdered cinnamon, ground cloves and grated nutmeg with the flour mixture in the recipe for American cookies.

ALMOND COOKIES

Add 25 gm (1 oz) finely chopped blanched almonds and the grated rind of a half a lemon to the recipe for cinnamon cookies.

COFFEE COOLERS

HONEY AND ORANGE CREAM COFFEE

METRIC
1 orange
568 ml black coffee
2 tablespoons clear honey

IMPERIAL
1 orange
1 pint black coffee
2 tablespoons clear honey

Strain juice of the orange into hot black coffee and sweeten with honey. Chill. Serve in glasses with double cream floating on top and decorate with grated orange rind.

VIENNESE VELVET

Fill two-thirds of a tall glass with vanilla flavoured ice cream. Pour over hot black coffee and top with lightly whipped cream.

MOCHA ICE CREAM SODA

Quarter fill a tall glass with chocolate or vanilla flavoured ice cream. Add 2 dessertspoonfuls strong black coffee. Fill up with soda water.

AMERICAN MEASURES

American measures are given by volume and weight using standard cups and spoons.

US Standard Measuring Spoons and Cups

1 tablespoon = 3 teaspoons = ½ fluid ounce = 14.2 ml
2 tablespoons = 1 fluid ounce = 28 ml
4 tablespoons = ¼ cup
5 tablespoons = ⅓ cup
8 tablespoons = ½ cup
10 tablespoons = ⅝ cup (i.e. ⅔ approx.)
12 tablespoons = ¾ cup
16 tablespoons = 2 cups = 8 fluid ounces = ½ US pint
32 tablespoons = 2 cups = 16 fluid ounces = 1 US pint.

Metric (Imperial)	American
1 teaspoon	1 teaspoon
1 tablespoon	1 tablespoon
1½ teaspoons	2 tablespoons
2 tablespoons	3 tablespoons
3 tablespoons	¼ (scant) cup
4 tablespoons	5 tablespoons
5 tablespoons	6 tablespoons
5½ tablespoons	7 tablespoons
6 tablespoons (scant ¼ pint)	½ cup
¼ pint	⅔ cup
scant ½ pint	1 cup
½ pint (10 fl oz)	1¼ cups
¾ pint (15 fl oz)	scant 2 cups
⅘ pint (16 fl oz)	2 cups (1 pint)
1 pint (20 fl oz)	2½ cups

Metric (Imperial)	American
flour, plain or self-raising	
15 gm (½ oz)	2 tablespoons
25 gm (1 oz)	1¼ cup
100/125 gm (4 oz)	1 cup
sugar, castor or granulated, brown (firmly packed)	
15 gm (1 oz)	2 tablespoons
100/125 gm (4 oz)	½ cup
200/225 gm (8 oz)	1 cup
butter, margarine, fat	
1 oz	2 tablespoons
225 gm (8 oz)	1 cup
150 gm (5 oz) shredded suet	1 cup

1 cup (American) contains approximately

100/125 gm (4 oz) grated cheese, 50 gm (2 oz) fresh breadcrumbs, 100 gm (4 oz) dried breadcrumbs,
100/125 gm (4 oz) pickled beetroot, button mushrooms, shelled peas, red/blackcurrants, 5 oz strawberries,
175 gm (6 oz) raisins, currants, sultans, chopped candied peel, stoned dates,
225 gm (8 oz) glacé cherries, 150 gm (5 oz) shelled whole walnuts, 100 gm (4 oz) chopped nuts,
75 gm (3 oz) dessicated coconut,
225 gm (8 oz) cottage cheese,
100/125 gm (4 oz) curry powder,
225 gm (8 oz) minced raw meat,
⅜ pint (7½ fl oz) cream.

INDEX